SET-1

1. Hello World:

```php
<?php
  echo "Hello, World!";
?>
```

2. Variables and Data Types:

```php
<?php
  $name = "John";
  $age = 25;
  $height = 5.9;

  echo "Name: $name, Age: $age, Height: $height";
?>
```

3. Arithmetic Operations:

```php
<?php
```

```php
  $num1 = 10;

  $num2 = 5;


  $sum = $num1 + $num2;

  $difference = $num1 - $num2;

  $product = $num1 * $num2;

  $quotient = $num1 / $num2;


  echo "Sum: $sum, Difference: $difference, Product: $product, Quotient: $quotient";

?>
```

4. Conditional Statements:

```php
<?php
  $score = 75;

  if ($score >= 60) {
   echo "Passed";
  } else {
   echo "Failed";
  }
?>
```

5. Looping (for):

```php
<?php
 for ($i = 1; $i <= 5; $i++) {
   echo "$i ";
 }
?>
```

6. Arrays:

```php
<?php
 $fruits = array("Apple", "Banana", "Orange");

 foreach ($fruits as $fruit) {
   echo "$fruit ";
 }
?>
```

7. Functions:

```php
<?php
 function add($a, $b) {
   return $a + $b;
 }
```

```php
$result = add(3, 4);
echo "Result: $result";
?>
```

8. String Manipulation:

```php
<?php
$text = "Hello, PHP";

echo strtoupper($text);  // Convert to uppercase
echo strtolower($text);  // Convert to lowercase
echo strlen($text);      // String length
echo str_replace("PHP", "World", $text); // Replace substring
?>
```

9. Form Handling (GET method):

```html
<!DOCTYPE html>
<html>
<body>

<form method="get" action="process.php">
  Name: <input type="text" name="name">
  <input type="submit" value="Submit">
```

```html
</form>

</body>
</html>
```

`process.php`:

```php
<?php
  $name = $_GET['name'];
  echo "Hello, $name!";
?>
```

10. File Handling:

```php
<?php
  $file = fopen("example.txt", "w");
  fwrite($file, "Hello, PHP!");
  fclose($file);

  $contents = file_get_contents("example.txt");
  echo $contents;
?>
```

SET - 2

11. Associative Arrays:

```php
<?php
 $person = array(
  "name" => "Alice",
  "age" => 30,
  "city" => "Wonderland"
 );


 echo "Name: " . $person["name"] . ", Age: " . $person["age"] . ", City: " . $person["city"];
?>
```

12. Switch Statement:

```php
<?php
 $day = "Monday";

 switch ($day) {
  case "Monday":
   echo "It's the start of the week.";
   break;
  case "Friday":
   echo "It's almost the weekend!";
   break;
  default:
```

```php
    echo "It's a regular day.";
  }
?>
```

13. Cookies:

```php
<?php
  setcookie("user", "John Doe", time() + 3600, "/");

  echo "Cookie is set.";
  echo "User: " . $_COOKIE["user"];
?>
```

14. Sessions:

```php
<?php
  session_start();

  $_SESSION["username"] = "admin";

  echo "Session is set.";
  echo "Username: " . $_SESSION["username"];
?>
```

15. Date and Time:

```php
<?php
  echo "Current Date: " . date("Y-m-d");
  echo "Current Time: " . date("H:i:s");
?>
```

16. Regular Expressions:

```php
<?php
  $email = "user@example.com";

  if (preg_match("/^[a-zA-Z0-9._-]+@[a-zA-Z0-9.-]+\.[a-zA-Z]{2,4}$/", $email)) {
    echo "Valid email address.";
  } else {
    echo "Invalid email address.";
  }
?>
```

17. Error Handling:

```php
<?php
  // Error reporting
```

```php
error_reporting(E_ERROR | E_WARNING | E_PARSE);

// Triggering an error
echo $undefinedVariable;
?>
```

18. Object-Oriented Programming (OOP):

```php
<?php
  class Car {
    public $brand;
    public $model;

    public function __construct($brand, $model) {
      $this->brand = $brand;
      $this->model = $model;
    }

    public function displayInfo() {
      echo "Brand: $this->brand, Model: $this->model";
    }
  }

  $myCar = new Car("Toyota", "Camry");
  $myCar->displayInfo();
```

```php
?>
```

19. JSON Handling:

```php
<?php
  $data = '{"name":"Bob","age":25,"city":"New York"}';
  $decodedData = json_decode($data);


  echo "Name: " . $decodedData->name . ", Age: " . $decodedData->age . ", City: " . $decodedData->city;
?>
```

20. Database Connection (MySQLi):

```php
<?php
  $servername = "localhost";
  $username = "root";
  $password = "";
  $dbname = "exampleDB";


  $conn = new mysqli($servername, $username, $password, $dbname);


  if ($conn->connect_error) {
    die("Connection failed: " . $conn->connect_error);
  }
```

```php
echo "Connected successfully";
$conn->close();
?>
```

SET – 3

21. File Upload:

```html
<!DOCTYPE html>
<html>
<body>

<form action="upload.php" method="post" enctype="multipart/form-data">
  Select file to upload:
  <input type="file" name="fileToUpload" id="fileToUpload">
  <input type="submit" value="Upload File" name="submit">
</form>

</body>
</html>
```

In `upload.php`:

```php
<?php
$target_dir = "uploads/";
$target_file = $target_dir . basename($_FILES["fileToUpload"]["name"]);
$uploadOk = 1;

if (move_uploaded_file($_FILES["fileToUpload"]["tmp_name"], $target_file)) {
  echo "The file ". htmlspecialchars(basename($_FILES["fileToUpload"]["name"])). " has been uploaded.";
} else {
  echo "Sorry, there was an error uploading your file.";
}
?>
```

22. Pagination (using GET parameters):

```php
<?php
$itemsPerPage = 10;
$currentPage = isset($_GET['page']) ? $_GET['page'] : 1;

$start = ($currentPage - 1) * $itemsPerPage;
$end = $start + $itemsPerPage;

// Fetch and display items from $start to $end
?>
```

23. CURL Request:

```php
<?php
 $url = "https://api.example.com/data";
 $ch = curl_init($url);

 curl_setopt($ch, CURLOPT_RETURNTRANSFER, true);
 $result = curl_exec($ch);

 curl_close($ch);

 echo $result;
?>
```

24. Sending Email:

```php
<?php
 $to = "recipient@example.com";
 $subject = "Test Email";
 $message = "This is a test email.";

 mail($to, $subject, $message);
 echo "Email sent.";
?>
```

25. Dynamic Image Creation:

```php
<?php
  header("Content-type: image/png");

  $image = imagecreate(200, 100);
  $bgColor = imagecolorallocate($image, 255, 255, 255);
  $textColor = imagecolorallocate($image, 0, 0, 0);

  imagestring($image, 4, 50, 40, "PHP", $textColor);
  imagepng($image);
  imagedestroy($image);
?>
```

26. GD Library for Image Manipulation:

```php
<?php
  $image = imagecreatefromjpeg("input.jpg");
  $rotate = imagerotate($image, 45, 0);

  header('Content-Type: image/jpeg');
  imagejpeg($rotate);
```

```php
 imagedestroy($image);
 imagedestroy($rotate);
?>
```

27. CSV File Handling:

```php
<?php
 $csvFile = fopen("data.csv", "r");

 while (($data = fgetcsv($csvFile, 1000, ",")) !== FALSE) {
   echo "Name: $data[0], Age: $data[1], City: $data[2] <br>";
 }

 fclose($csvFile);
?>
```

28. XML Parsing:

```php
<?php
 $xmlString = '<root><element1>Value 1</element1><element2>Value
2</element2></root>';
 $xml = simplexml_load_string($xmlString);

 echo "Element 1: " . $xml->element1 . "<br>";
 echo "Element 2: " . $xml->element2 . "<br>";
```

```php
?>
```

29. JWT (JSON Web Token) Handling:

```php
<?php
$payload = array("user_id" => 123, "username" => "john_doe");
$secretKey = "my_secret_key";


$token = jwt_encode($payload, $secretKey);
echo "JWT: $token";


$decodedPayload = jwt_decode($token, $secretKey);
echo "Decoded Payload: ";
print_r($decodedPayload);
?>
```

30. Basic Authentication:

```php
<?php
$username = "admin";
$password = "secret";


if ($_SERVER['PHP_AUTH_USER'] == $username &&
$_SERVER['PHP_AUTH_PW'] == $password) {

  echo "Authentication successful!";
```

```php
  } else {

    header('WWW-Authenticate: Basic realm="My Realm"');

    header('HTTP/1.0 401 Unauthorized');

    echo "Authentication failed!";

  }
?>
```

SET – 4

31. URL Parameters Handling:

```php
<?php
  $name = isset($_GET['name']) ? $_GET['name'] : 'Guest';

  echo "Hello, $name!";
?>
```

32. Recursive Function:

```php
<?php
  function factorial($n) {
    if ($n === 0 || $n === 1) {
      return 1;
    } else {
```

```php
    return $n * factorial($n - 1);
  }
}


echo "Factorial of 5 is " . factorial(5);
?>
```

33. Simple Session Authentication:

```php
<?php
  session_start();

  if (isset($_SESSION['user'])) {
    echo "Welcome, " . $_SESSION['user'] . "!";
  } else {
    header("Location: login.php");
    exit();
  }
?>
```

34. Basic CRUD Operations with MySQL:

```php
<?php
  $conn = mysqli_connect("localhost", "username", "password", "database");
```

```php
// Insert
mysqli_query($conn, "INSERT INTO users (name, email) VALUES ('John Doe', 'john@example.com')");

// Update
mysqli_query($conn, "UPDATE users SET name = 'Jane Doe' WHERE id = 1");

// Select
$result = mysqli_query($conn, "SELECT * FROM users");
while ($row = mysqli_fetch_assoc($result)) {
  echo "Name: " . $row['name'] . ", Email: " . $row['email'] . "<br>";
}

// Delete
mysqli_query($conn, "DELETE FROM users WHERE id = 1");

mysqli_close($conn);
?>
```

35. Using Composer Packages:

```php
<?php
require 'vendor/autoload.php';

use Monolog\Logger;
```

```php
use Monolog\Handler\StreamHandler;

$log = new Logger('name');
$log->pushHandler(new StreamHandler('path/to/your.log',
Logger::WARNING));

$log->warning('This is a warning message');
?>
```

36. Sending JSON Response:

```php
<?php
$data = array("name" => "John Doe", "age" => 25, "city" => "New York");
header('Content-Type: application/json');
echo json_encode($data);
?>
```

37. Fetching Remote Content (Web Scraping):

```php
<?php
$url = "https://www.example.com";
$content = file_get_contents($url);

echo $content;
?>
```

38. Handling Multiple Forms on the Same Page:

```php
<?php
 if ($_SERVER["REQUEST_METHOD"] == "POST") {
  if (isset($_POST['form1'])) {
   // Process form 1
  } elseif (isset($_POST['form2'])) {
   // Process form 2
  }
 }
?>
```

39. Dynamic Page Generation:

```php
<?php
 $page = isset($_GET['page']) ? $_GET['page'] : 'home';

 switch ($page) {
  case 'home':
   echo "Welcome to the home page!";
   break;
  case 'about':
   echo "Learn more about us!";
```

```php
    break;
  // Add more cases for other pages
  default:
    echo "Page not found!";
 }
?>
```

40. Creating a RESTful API Endpoint:

```php
<?php
 $method = $_SERVER['REQUEST_METHOD'];

 if ($method == 'GET') {
  // Retrieve data
  // Return data as JSON
 } elseif ($method == 'POST') {
  // Process incoming data
  // Save data to the database
 } else {
  header('HTTP/1.1 405 Method Not Allowed');
  echo "Method Not Allowed";
 }
?>
```

41. Handling AJAX Requests:

```php
<?php
 if ($_SERVER['REQUEST_METHOD'] === 'POST' && isset($_POST['data'])) {
   $data = $_POST['data'];
   // Process the data and send a response
   echo "Received data: $data";
 } else {
   echo "Invalid request";
 }
?>
```

42. Creating and Using a Simple Class:

```php
<?php
 class Dog {
   public $name;

   public function bark() {
     return "Woof!";
   }
 }
```

```php
$myDog = new Dog();
$myDog->name = "Buddy";
echo $myDog->name . " says: " . $myDog->bark();
?>
```

43. Using Traits in PHP:

```php
<?php
trait Log {
  public function logMessage($message) {
    echo "Log: $message";
  }
}

class User {
  use Log;
}

$user = new User();
$user->logMessage("User logged in.");
?>
```

44. Creating a Simple Middleware:

```php
<?php
function middlewareExample($next) {
    // Perform actions before the main logic
    echo "Executing middleware before main logic. ";

    // Call the next middleware or main logic
    $next();

    // Perform actions after the main logic
    echo "Executing middleware after main logic. ";
}

function mainLogic() {
    echo "Main logic executed. ";
}

// Using the middleware
middlewareExample('mainLogic');
?>
```

45. Handling File Downloads:

```php
<?php
$file = 'example.pdf';
```

```php
header('Content-Type: application/pdf');
header('Content-Disposition: attachment; filename="' . basename($file) . '"');
readfile($file);
?>
```

46. Custom Error Handling:

```php
<?php
function customError($errno, $errstr) {
  echo "Error: [$errno] $errstr";
}

set_error_handler("customError");

// Trigger an error
echo $undefinedVariable;
?>
```

47. Using PDO for Database Access:

```php
<?php
try {
  $conn = new PDO("mysql:host=localhost;dbname=mydatabase", "username", "password");
  $conn->setAttribute(PDO::ATTR_ERRMODE, PDO::ERRMODE_EXCEPTION);
```

```php
  $result = $conn->query("SELECT * FROM users");

  foreach ($result as $row) {

    echo "Name: " . $row['name'] . ", Email: " . $row['email'] . "<br>";

  }


  $conn = null;

} catch (PDOException $e) {

  echo "Error: " . $e->getMessage();

}

?>
```

48. Using Composer for Autoloading Classes:

```php
<?php
  require 'vendor/autoload.php';


  use MyNamespace\MyClass;


  $obj = new MyClass();

  $obj->doSomething();

?>
```

49. Handling Sessions Securely:

```php
<?php
  session_start();


  if (isset($_SESSION['user']) && hash_equals($_SESSION['token'], $_POST['token'])) {
    // Process data
    echo "Data processed successfully.";
  } else {
    echo "Invalid session or token.";
  }
?>
```

50. Creating a Basic Middleware Stack:

```php
<?php
  function middleware1($next) {
    echo "Middleware 1 before. ";
    $next();
    echo "Middleware 1 after. ";
  }


  function middleware2($next) {
    echo "Middleware 2 before. ";
    $next();
    echo "Middleware 2 after. ";
```

```php
}

function mainLogic() {
  echo "Main logic executed. ";
}

// Using a middleware stack
$middlewareStack = ['middleware1', 'middleware2'];
$next = 'mainLogic';

foreach ($middlewareStack as $middleware) {
  $next = function () use ($middleware, $next) {
    return $middleware($next);
  };
}

$next();
?>
```

SET – 6

51. Handling JSON Web Tokens (JWT) with a Library:

```php
<?php
  require 'vendor/autoload.php';
```

```php
use Firebase\JWT\JWT;


$key = "your_secret_key";
$payload = array(
  "user_id" => 123,
  "username" => "john_doe"
);


$token = JWT::encode($payload, $key);
echo "JWT: $token";


$decodedPayload = JWT::decode($token, $key, array('HS256'));
echo "Decoded Payload: ";
print_r($decodedPayload);
?>
```

52. Generating Random Password:

```php
<?php
 function generateRandomPassword($length = 8) {
   $characters =
'0123456789abcdefghijklmnopqrstuvwxyzABCDEFGHIJKLMNOPQRSTUVWXYZ';
   $password = '';


   for ($i = 0; $i < $length; $i++) {
```

```php
    $password .= $characters[rand(0, strlen($characters) - 1)];
  }


  return $password;
}


echo "Random Password: " . generateRandomPassword();
?>
```

53. Using PHP Sessions to Prevent Form Resubmission:

```php
<?php
  session_start();


  if ($_SERVER['REQUEST_METHOD'] == 'POST') {
    // Process the form data
    $_SESSION['token'] = bin2hex(random_bytes(32));
    // Additional processing...
  }
?>
```

54. Using the SimpleXML Extension for XML Parsing:

```php
<?php
```

```php
$xmlString = '<root><element1>Value 1</element1><element2>Value 2</element2></root>';

$xml = simplexml_load_string($xmlString);


echo "Element 1: " . $xml->element1 . "<br>";

echo "Element 2: " . $xml->element2 . "<br>";
?>
```

55. Implementing a Basic MVC Structure:

```php
<?php
// Assuming a folder structure with controllers, models, and views
require 'controllers/HomeController.php';

require 'models/HomeModel.php';

require 'views/HomeView.php';


$model = new HomeModel();

$view = new HomeView($model);

$controller = new HomeController($model, $view);


$controller->show();
?>
```

56. Creating a Simple RESTful API Endpoint with Slim Framework:

```php
<?php
  require 'vendor/autoload.php';


  $app = new \Slim\App();


  $app->get('/api/data', function ($request, $response) {
    $data = array("name" => "John Doe", "age" => 25, "city" => "New York");
    return $response->withJson($data);
  });


  $app->run();
?>
```

57. Using the Guzzle HTTP Client for API Requests:

```php
<?php
  require 'vendor/autoload.php';

  use GuzzleHttp\Client;

  $client = new Client();
  $response = $client->request('GET', 'https://api.example.com/data');

  echo $response->getBody();
?>
```

58. Image Upload and Validation:

```php
<?php
 if ($_SERVER['REQUEST_METHOD'] == 'POST' && isset($_FILES['image'])) {
   $target_dir = "uploads/";
   $target_file = $target_dir . basename($_FILES["image"]["name"]);
   $uploadOk = 1;

   // Validate image file
   $imageFileType = strtolower(pathinfo($target_file, PATHINFO_EXTENSION));
   if ($imageFileType != "jpg" && $imageFileType != "png" && $imageFileType != "jpeg") {
    echo "Invalid file format.";
    $uploadOk = 0;
   }

  if ($uploadOk == 1) {
    move_uploaded_file($_FILES["image"]["tmp_name"], $target_file);
    echo "Image uploaded successfully.";
   }
 }
?>
```

59. Working with Composer Scripts:

```php
<?php
// In composer.json
// "scripts": {
//   "post-install-cmd": [
//     "php -r \"echo 'Installation completed.';\""
//   ]
// }
?>
```

60. Creating a Basic Authentication System with Password Hashing:

```php
<?php
// Assume registration and login logic with password hashing
$password = "user_password";
$hashedPassword = password_hash($password, PASSWORD_DEFAULT);

// During login
$userEnteredPassword = "user_password";
if (password_verify($userEnteredPassword, $hashedPassword)) {
  echo "Password is correct.";
} else {
  echo "Password is incorrect.";
}
?>
```

SET – 7

61. Creating and Using Namespaces:

```php
<?php
 namespace MyNamespace;

 class MyClass {
   public function doSomething() {
     echo "Doing something in MyNamespace.";
   }
 }


 $obj = new MyClass();
 $obj->doSomething();
?>
```

62. Implementing a Singleton Design Pattern:

```php
<?php
 class Singleton {
   private static $instance;
```

```php
    private function __construct() {
      // Private constructor to prevent instantiation
    }


    public static function getInstance() {
      if (!isset(self::$instance)) {
        self::$instance = new self();
      }
      return self::$instance;
    }
}


  $singletonInstance = Singleton::getInstance();
?>
```

63. Using the SPL (Standard PHP Library) Classes:

```php
<?php
  $stack = new SplStack();
  $stack->push("Item 1");
  $stack->push("Item 2");

  echo "Top item: " . $stack->top() . "<br>";

  $queue = new SplQueue();
```

```php
$queue->enqueue("Task 1");

$queue->enqueue("Task 2");


echo "Front task: " . $queue->dequeue() . "<br>";

?>
```


64. Handling Cross-Origin Resource Sharing (CORS):

```php
<?php
  header("Access-Control-Allow-Origin: *");

  header("Access-Control-Allow-Methods: GET, POST, OPTIONS");

  header("Access-Control-Allow-Headers: Content-Type");


  // Handle CORS preflight requests
  if ($_SERVER['REQUEST_METHOD'] == 'OPTIONS') {
   http_response_code(204);
   exit();
  }


  // Process the main request
  // ...
?>
```


65. Creating and Using Traits with Abstract Classes:

```php
<?php
trait Log {
  public function logMessage($message) {
    echo "Log: $message";
  }
}


abstract class Logger {
  use Log;

  abstract public function log($message);
}


class FileLogger extends Logger {
  public function log($message) {
    $this->logMessage("File: $message");
  }
}


$fileLogger = new FileLogger();
$fileLogger->log("An important message");
?>
```

66. Using the DOMDocument Class for HTML Manipulation:

```php
<?php
$html = '<div><p>Hello, <b>PHP</b>!</p></div>';
$dom = new DOMDocument();
$dom->loadHTML($html);


$boldText = $dom->getElementsByTagName('b')->item(0)->nodeValue;
echo "Bold Text: $boldText";
?>
```

67. Creating a Simple Command-Line Script:

```php
<?php
// command-line-script.php
if ($argc < 2) {
  echo "Usage: php command-line-script.php [argument]\n";
  exit(1);
}


$argument = $argv[1];
echo "Argument: $argument\n";
?>
```

68. Handling Long-Running Processes with Gearman:

```php
<?php
$client = new GearmanClient();

$client->addServer();


$task = $client->addTask("longRunningTask", "data");


$client->runTasks();


if ($task->isSuccessful()) {
  echo "Task completed successfully.";
} else {
  echo "Task failed.";
}
?>
```

69. Using the Memcached Extension for Caching:

```php
<?php
$memcached = new Memcached();
$memcached->addServer('localhost', 11211);


$key = 'example_key';
$data = $memcached->get($key);
```

```php
if ($data === false) {

  // Data not in cache, fetch from the source and store in cache

  $data = fetchDataFromSource();

  $memcached->set($key, $data, 3600); // Cache for 1 hour

}


  echo "Data: $data";

?>
```

70. Creating a Basic WebSocket Server with Ratchet:

```php
<?php
  require 'vendor/autoload.php';


  use Ratchet\MessageComponentInterface;

  use Ratchet\ConnectionInterface;

  use Ratchet\Server\IoServer;

  use

Ratchet\Http\HttpServer;

  use Ratchet\WebSocket\WsServer;


  class MyWebSocketServer implements MessageComponentInterface {

    public function onOpen(ConnectionInterface $conn) {

      // Connection opened
```

```php
        echo "New connection! ({$conn->resourceId})\n";
    }

    public function onMessage(ConnectionInterface $from, $msg) {
        // Message received
        echo "Message from {$from->resourceId}: $msg\n";

        // Broadcast the message to all clients
        foreach ($this->clients as $client) {
            $client->send($msg);
        }
    }

    public function onClose(ConnectionInterface $conn) {
        // Connection closed
        echo "Connection {$conn->resourceId} has disconnected\n";
    }

    public function onError(ConnectionInterface $conn, \Exception $e) {
        // Error occurred
        echo "An error has occurred: {$e->getMessage()}\n";
        $conn->close();
    }
}

$server = IoServer::factory(
```

```php
    new HttpServer(
      new WsServer(
        new MyWebSocketServer()
      )
    ),
    8080
  );

  $server->run();
?>
```

SET – 8

71. Working with DateTime:

```php
<?php
  $currentDate = new DateTime();
  echo "Current Date: " . $currentDate->format('Y-m-d H:i:s') . "<br>";

  $futureDate = new DateTime('+1 week');
  echo "Future Date: " . $futureDate->format('Y-m-d H:i:s');
?>
```

72. Creating and Using Composer Packages:

```php
<?php
  // Create a new Composer package using `composer init`
  // Define autoload settings in composer.json
  // Use the package in another project
  require 'vendor/autoload.php';

  use MyPackage\MyClass;

  $obj = new MyClass();
  $obj->doSomething();
?>
```

73. Using PHP Generators:

```php
<?php
  function generateNumbers($max) {
   for ($i = 1; $i <= $max; $i++) {
     yield $i;
   }
  }

  foreach (generateNumbers(5) as $number) {
   echo $number . ' ';
  }
```

?>

74. Creating a Basic REST API with Slim Framework:

```php
<?php
  require 'vendor/autoload.php';


  $app = new \Slim\App();


  $app->get('/api/data', function ($request, $response) {
    $data = array("name" => "John Doe", "age" => 25, "city" => "New York");
    return $response->withJson($data);
  });


  $app->run();
?>
```

75. Using Laravel Eloquent ORM:

```php
<?php
  use Illuminate\Database\Eloquent\Model;


  class User extends Model {
    protected $table = 'users';
```

```php
}

$user = User::find(1);
echo "User ID: " . $user->id . ", Name: " . $user->name;
?>
```

76. Creating a Simple CAPTCHA Image:

```php
<?php
session_start();

$image = imagecreatetruecolor(100, 30);
$background_color = imagecolorallocate($image, 255, 255, 255);
$text_color = imagecolorallocate($image, 0, 0, 0);

$random_string = substr(md5(rand()), 0, 5);
$_SESSION['captcha'] = $random_string;

imagestring($image, 5, 10, 5, $random_string, $text_color);

header('Content-Type: image/png');
imagepng($image);
imagedestroy($image);
?>
```

77. Using Guzzle for HTTP Requests with Promises:

```php
<?php
 require 'vendor/autoload.php';

 use GuzzleHttp\Client;
 use GuzzleHttp\Promise;

 $client = new Client();

 $promises = [
   'promise1' => $client->getAsync('https://api.example.com/endpoint1'),
   'promise2' => $client->getAsync('https://api.example.com/endpoint2'),
 ];

 $results = Promise\settle($promises)->wait();

 foreach ($results as $key => $result) {
   echo "$key: " . $result['value']->getBody() . "<br>";
 }
?>
```

78. Using Symfony Console Component:

```php
<?php
  require 'vendor/autoload.php';

  use Symfony\Component\Console\Application;
  use Symfony\Component\Console\Command\Command;
  use Symfony\Component\Console\Input\InputInterface;
  use Symfony\Component\Console\Output\OutputInterface;

  class MyCommand extends Command {
   protected function configure() {
    $this->setName('my:command')
      ->setDescription('My custom command');
   }

   protected function execute(InputInterface $input, OutputInterface $output) {
    $output->writeln('Executing my command...');
   }
  }

  $application = new Application();
  $application->add(new MyCommand());
  $application->run();
?>
```

79. Handling Form Submissions with CSRF Protection:

```php
<?php
session_start();

if ($_SERVER['REQUEST_METHOD'] === 'POST' && isset($_POST['token'])) {
  if ($_POST['token'] === $_SESSION['token']) {
    // Process the form data
    echo "Form submitted successfully.";
  } else {
    echo "CSRF token mismatch.";
  }
}
?>
```

80. Using PHPUnit for Unit Testing:

```php
<?php
class MyTest extends PHPUnit\Framework\TestCase {
  public function testAddition() {
    $result = 2 + 2;
    $this->assertEquals(4, $result);
  }

  public function testStringConcatenation() {
    $string = "Hello" . " " . "World";
```

```php
    $this->assertEquals("Hello World", $string);
  }

 }
?>
```

SET – 9

81. Creating a Basic Dependency Injection Container:

```php
<?php
 class Container {
   private $services = [];

   public function addService($name, $callback) {
    $this->services[$name] = $callback;
   }

   public function getService($name) {
    if (isset($this->services[$name])) {
     return call_user_func($this->services[$name]);
    }
   }
 }

 // Usage
```

```php
$container = new Container();

$container->addService('logger', function () {

  return new Logger();

});


$logger = $container->getService('logger');

$logger->log('Dependency Injection Container example.');

?>
```

82. Implementing PSR-4 Autoloading with Composer:

```php
<?php
  // In composer.json
  // "autoload": {
  //   "psr-4": {
  //     "MyNamespace\\": "src/"
  //   }
  // }


  // File structure
  // src/MyNamespace/MyClass.php


  // MyClass.php
  namespace MyNamespace;
```

```php
class MyClass {
  // Class implementation
 }
?>
```

83. Using Flysystem for File System Abstraction:

```php
<?php
  require 'vendor/autoload.php';

  use League\Flysystem\Filesystem;
  use League\Flysystem\Adapter\Local;

  $adapter = new Local(__DIR__.'/path/to/files');
  $filesystem = new Filesystem($adapter);

  $contents = $filesystem->read('example.txt');
  echo "File Contents: $contents";
?>
```

84. Creating a Simple JSON-RPC Server:

```php
<?php
  $request = json_decode(file_get_contents('php://input'), true);
```

```php
if (isset($request['method'])) {

  $method = $request['method'];

  $params = $request['params'] ?? [];


  switch ($method) {

    case 'add':

     $result = array_sum($params);

     break;

    default:

     $result = 'Method not found';

  }


  echo json_encode(['result' => $result]);

} else {

  echo json_encode(['error' => 'Invalid Request']);

}

?>
```

85. Handling Environment Variables with Dotenv:

```php
<?php

  require 'vendor/autoload.php';


  $dotenv = Dotenv\Dotenv::createImmutable(__DIR__);
```

```php
$dotenv->load();

$databaseHost = $_ENV['DB_HOST'];
$databaseUser = $_ENV['DB_USER'];
$databasePassword = $_ENV['DB_PASSWORD'];

// Use variables as needed
?>
```

86. Using Monolog for Logging:

```php
<?php
require 'vendor/autoload.php';

use Monolog\Logger;
use Monolog\Handler\StreamHandler;

$log = new Logger('name');
$log->pushHandler(new StreamHandler('path/to/your.log',
Logger::WARNING));

$log->warning('This is a warning message');
?>
```

87. Creating a Basic PSR-7 HTTP Message with Zend Diactoros:

```php
<?php
require 'vendor/autoload.php';

use Zend\Diactoros\Response;
use Zend\Diactoros\ServerRequestFactory;

$request = ServerRequestFactory::fromGlobals();
$response = new Response();

$response->getBody()->write('Hello, PSR-7!');
echo $response->getBody();
?>
```

88. Using Twig for Template Rendering:

```php
<?php
require 'vendor/autoload.php';

use Twig\Environment;
use Twig\Loader\FilesystemLoader;

$loader = new FilesystemLoader('/path/to/templates');
$twig = new Environment($loader);
```

```php
$template = $twig->load('template.twig');
echo $template->render(['name' => 'John']);
?>
```

89. Handling Webhooks with PHP:

```php
<?php
$payload = json_decode(file_get_contents('php://input'), true);

if (isset($payload['event'])) {
  $event = $payload['event'];

  switch ($event) {
    case 'payment.success':
      // Handle successful payment
      break;
    case 'user.signup':
      // Handle user signup
      break;
    default:
      // Handle other events
  }
}
?>
```

90. Creating a Simple URL Shortener:

```php
<?php
  // Assume using a database for storing URLs
  $url = $_GET['url'];
  $shortCode = generateShortCode();

  // Save $url and $shortCode to the database

  echo "Shortened URL: http://example.com/$shortCode";
?>
```

SET – 10

91. Using Opis Closure for Serializable Closures:

```php
<?php
  require 'vendor/autoload.php';

  use Opis\Closure\SerializableClosure;

  $addFunction = function($a, $b) {
    return $a + $b;
  };
```

```php
$serializedClosure = SerializableClosure::serialize($addFunction);

$unserializedClosure = SerializableClosure::unserialize($serializedClosure);

echo $unserializedClosure(2, 3); // Outputs 5
?>
```

92. Using Fractal for API Transformation:

```php
<?php
require 'vendor/autoload.php';

use League\Fractal\Manager;
use League\Fractal\Resource\Item;
use League\Fractal\Serializer\DataArraySerializer;

$data = ['id' => 1, 'name' => 'John Doe'];

$fractal = new Manager();
$fractal->setSerializer(new DataArraySerializer());

$resource = new Item($data, function($data) {
  return $data;
});
```

```php
$array = $fractal->createData($resource)->toArray();

print_r($array);
?>
```

93. Creating a Basic File Upload Form:

```php
<?php
if ($_SERVER['REQUEST_METHOD'] === 'POST' && isset($_FILES['file'])) {
  $target_dir = "uploads/";
  $target_file = $target_dir . basename($_FILES["file"]["name"]);

  if (move_uploaded_file($_FILES["file"]["tmp_name"], $target_file)) {
    echo "File uploaded successfully.";
  } else {
    echo "Error uploading file.";
  }
}
?>
```

94. Implementing Rate Limiting with Redis:

```php
<?php
require 'vendor/autoload.php';
```

```php
use Predis\Client;

$redis = new Client();

$ip = $_SERVER['REMOTE_ADDR'];
$key = "rate_limit:$ip";
$limit = 100; // Requests per minute

$currentRequests = $redis->incr($key);
$redis->expire($key, 60); // Expire in 60 seconds

if ($currentRequests > $limit) {
  http_response_code(429); // Too Many Requests
  echo "Rate limit exceeded.";
  exit();
}

// Process the request
echo "Request processed successfully.";
?>
```

95. Creating a Basic CMS with Laravel:

```php
<?php
```

```php
// Laravel installation and setup

// Define routes, controllers, models, and views


// Example Route

Route::get('/posts', 'PostController@index');


// Example Controller

class PostController extends Controller {

  public function index() {

    $posts = Post::all();

    return view('posts.index', compact('posts'));

  }

}


// Example Model

class Post extends Model {

  // Model implementation

}


// Example View

// resources/views/posts/index.blade.php

// ...

?>
```

96. Implementing Two-Factor Authentication (2FA):

```php
<?php
// Use a 2FA library like "RobThree/TwoFactorAuth"
require 'vendor/autoload.php';

use RobThree\Auth\TwoFactorAuth;

$tfa = new TwoFactorAuth('MyApp');

// Generate a secret key for the user
$secretKey = $tfa->createSecret();

// Display QR code for user to scan
echo '<img src="' . $tfa->getQRCodeImageAsDataUri('User', $secretKey) . '">';

// Verify user's input
$isValid = $tfa->verifyCode($secretKey, $_POST['verification_code']);

if ($isValid) {
  echo "Two-factor authentication successful.";
} else {
  echo "Invalid verification code.";
}
?>
```

97. Creating a Simple Real-Time Chat Application with WebSocket:

```php
<?php
// Using Ratchet library for WebSocket
require 'vendor/autoload.php';

use Ratchet\MessageComponentInterface;
use Ratchet\ConnectionInterface;
use Ratchet\Server\IoServer;
use Ratchet\Http\HttpServer;
use Ratchet\WebSocket\WsServer;

class Chat implements MessageComponentInterface {
  // Implement WebSocket methods
  // ...
}

$server = IoServer::factory(
  new HttpServer(
   new WsServer(
    new Chat()
   )
  ),
  8080
);
```

```php
  $server->run();
?>
```

98. Handling Form Validation with Laravel:

```php
<?php
  // Laravel form validation example
  public function store(Request $request) {
    $validatedData = $request->validate([
      'name' => 'required|max:255',
      'email' => 'required|email|unique:users',
      'password' => 'required|min:8',
    ]);

    // Process the validated data
  }
?>
```

99. Using Guzzle Middleware for Request/Response Modification:

```php
<?php
  require 'vendor/autoload.php';

  use GuzzleHttp\Client;
```

```php
use GuzzleHttp\HandlerStack;
use GuzzleHttp\Middleware;

$stack = HandlerStack::create();

$stack->push(Middleware::mapRequest(function ($request) {
  // Modify request before sending
  // ...
  return $request;
}));

$stack->push(Middleware::mapResponse(function ($response) {
  // Modify response after receiving
  // ...
  return $response;
}));

$client = new Client(['handler' => $stack]);

// Make requests using $client
?>
```

100. Using PHP's Sodium Crypto Library for Secure Encryption:

```php
<?php
```

```php
// Requires PHP 7.2 or later with Sodium extension

$message = "This is a secret message";

$key = sodium_crypto_secretbox_keygen();

$nonce = random_bytes(SODIUM_CRYPTO_SECRETBOX_NONCEBYTES);


$encryptedMessage = sodium_crypto_secretbox($message, $nonce, $key);


// Send $encryptedMessage and $nonce to the recipient
// ...


$decryptedMessage = sodium_crypto_secretbox_open($encryptedMessage, $nonce, $key);


echo "Decrypted Message: $decryptedMessage";
?>
```

Thank You!